TOM HOLLAND

ACTING ★ SUPERSTAR

MEGAN BORGERT-SPANIOL

Big Buddy Books

An Imprint of Abdo Publishing
abdobooks.com

ABDOBOOKS.COM

Published by Abdo Publishing, a division of ABDO, PO Box 398166, Minneapolis, Minnesota 55439. Copyright © 2022 by Abdo Consulting Group, Inc. International copyrights reserved in all countries. No part of this book may be reproduced in any form without written permission from the publisher. Big Buddy Books™ is a trademark and logo of Abdo Publishing.

Printed in the United States of America, North Mankato, Minnesota

052021
092021

Design: Kelly Doudna, Mighty Media, Inc.
Production: Mighty Media, Inc.
Editor: Liz Salzmann
Cover Photograph: Shutterstock Images
Interior Photographs: David M. Benett/Getty Images, p. 7; Flickr, pp. 9, 23; Shutterstock Images, pp. 1, 5, 13, 15, 17, 19, 21, 25, 27, 28 (left), 29 (all); Wikimedia Commons, pp. 11, 28 (right)

Library of Congress Control Number: 2020949956

Publisher's Cataloging-in-Publication Data

Names: Borgert-Spaniol, Megan, author.
Title: Tom Holland: acting superstar / by Megan Borgert-Spaniol
Other title: acting superstar
Description: Minneapolis, Minnesota : Abdo Publishing, 2022 | Series: Superstars | Includes online resources and index.
Identifiers: ISBN 9781532195679 (lib. bdg.) | ISBN 9781098216405 (ebook)
Subjects: LCSH: Holland, Tom, 1996- --Juvenile literature. | Actors--Great Britain--Biography--Juvenile literature. | Motion picture actors and actresses--Great Britain--Biography--Juvenile literature. | Superhero films--Juvenile literature.
Classification: DDC 791.430--dc23

CONTENTS

Tom Holland ★★★★★★★★★★★★★★★★★★★★★★★ 4

Dance Class ★★★★★★★★★★★★★★★★★★★★★★★ 6

Billy Elliot ★★★★★★★★★★★★★★★★★★★★★★★ 8

First Movies ★★★★★★★★★★★★★★★★★★★★★★★ 12

Carpentry School ★★★★★★★★★★★★★★★★★★★★★★ 14

Dream Role ★★★★★★★★★★★★★★★★★★★★★★★ 16

Spider-Man ★★★★★★★★★★★★★★★★★★★★★★★ 20

Bright Future ★★★★★★★★★★★★★★★★★★★★★★★ 24

Timeline ★★★★★★★★★★★★★★★★★★★★★★★★ 28

Glossary ★★★★★★★★★★★★★★★★★★★★★★★★ 30

Online Resources ★★★★★★★★★★★★★★★★★★★★★ 31

Index ★★★★★★★★★★★★★★★★★★★★★★★★★ 32

TOM HOLLAND

Tom Holland is an English actor. He started acting when he was 12 years old. Later, he became famous for playing the superhero Spider-Man.

But Spider-Man isn't Holland's only character. He has played many different **roles**. He hopes to continue to try new ones!

As far as my future goes, I want to stretch myself as an actor.

Holland does a lot of his own movie stunts.

DANCE CLASS

Thomas Stanley Holland was born on June 1, 1996, near London, England. His mother, Nicola, is a **photographer**. His father, Dominic, is a **comedian** and author. Tom's three younger brothers are Harry, Sam, and Paddy.

When Tom was ten, he started **hip-hop** dance classes. The skills he learned there helped him earn his first acting **role**.

Tom with his family in 2018. *Left to right*: Tom, Dominic, Paddy, Nicola, Sam, Harry.

BILLY ELLIOT

In 2006, Tom's dance class performed at a festival. There, Tom caught the attention of a dance teacher. She told Tom he should **audition** for *Billy Elliot: The Musical*.

This play is about a boy who becomes a ballet dancer. Tom wanted a **role** in the play. So, he began learning ballet. He knew he had to be a good dancer to get a part.

Billy Elliot: The Musical was staged at the Victoria Palace Theatre in London.

After two years of training and several **auditions**, Tom's work paid off. In September 2008, he was finally chosen to play Billy Elliot. He performed this star **role** on stage for almost two years.

> I'm very happy I had that [ballet] training. It's been so valuable to my career, and I've used it on almost everything I've done since.

March 31, 2010, was *Billy Elliot: The Musical*'s fifth anniversary. That night, 18 other actors who played Billy over the years joined Tom (*second from left*) for a special finale.

FIRST MOVIES

Tom's theater run ended in 2010. But it wasn't long before he had another job. That summer, Tom filmed *The Impossible*. It is a movie about a family that gets caught in a **tsunami**. In 2013, Tom filmed *In the Heart of the Sea*. He played a sailor in this movie.

SUPERSTAR ★ SCOOP
The tsunami scenes in *The Impossible* were shot in a giant water tank. Tom was pulled through the water in a cart!

In *In the Heart of the Sea*, Tom (*left*) worked with (*left to right*) actors Benjamin Walker and Chris Hemsworth and director Ron Howard.

CARPENTRY SCHOOL

By 2014, Holland was feeling **confident** as an actor. But his parents wanted him to have a plan if acting didn't work out. So, they sent him to carpentry school.

Holland liked learning how to build. But he also kept **auditioning** for movies. One audition was for Marvel Comics superhero Spider-Man.

Holland's carpentry school was in Cardiff, the capital of Wales.

DREAM ROLE

The **audition** process for Spider-Man took more than five months. Holland left school to have more time to work on getting the **role**.

During the auditions, Holland read lines with actors Robert Downey Jr. and Chris Evans. Downey and Evans played superheroes Iron Man and Captain America. Holland would work closely with them if he got the part.

Robert Downey Jr. played Iron Man in more than ten movies.

Holland stood out during his **auditions**. His training in ballet and **hip-hop** showed in the way he moved. He could also do flips and other **gymnastics** skills.

In June 2015, Marvel Studios announced the big news. Holland would be playing Spider-Man!

SUPERSTAR ★ SCOOP
Holland first learned he got the Spider-Man part from an Instagram post. He later got a call from the president of Marvel Studios.

Holland was 19 when he got the part of Spider-Man. He was the youngest actor to ever play the superhero in a live-action movie.

SPIDER-MAN

Holland faced high expectations in his new **role**. Many actors had played Spider-Man in earlier movies. Holland had to prove he was a worthy Spider-Man.

Holland first played Spider-Man in the 2016 movie *Captain America: Civil War*. He appeared alongside other superheroes played by popular actors. But Holland stood out. Fans wanted to see more of the new Spider-Man!

In 2002, Tobey Maguire became the first actor to play Spider-Man in a major movie.

Spider-Man: Homecoming came out in 2017. In everyday life, Spider-Man is Peter Parker, a New York City high school student. His double life as Spider-Man is a secret. Fans loved Holland's fresh take on Parker and Spider-Man!

SUPERSTAR ★ SCOOP

To prepare for his **role** as Peter Parker, Holland attended a New York high school. He used a fake name. Even the teachers thought he was a real student!

Jon Watts (*right*) directed Holland in *Spider-Man: Homecoming*.

BRIGHT FUTURE

Over the next few years, Holland played Spider-Man in three more movies. These were *Avengers: Infinity War*, *Avengers: Endgame*, and *Spider-Man: Far from Home*.

A new Spider-Man movie was planned for 2021. Holland was happy to keep playing Spider-Man. But he also filmed two other movies that came out that year.

One of Holland's 2021 movies was *Chaos Walking*. Daisy Ridley was Holland's costar in the movie.

Looking ahead, Holland hoped to one day win an Academy Award. He also wanted to direct his own movie. In the meantime, his goal was to keep enjoying himself. "I really am having the time of my life," he said.

SUPERSTAR ★ SCOOP

Holland often gave away movie plots to the public by accident. So, the directors of *Avengers: Endgame* didn't give him a full **script**. He only received his own lines!

> **I really am nothing but grateful, and I've made friends for life along the way.**

Holland and Downey Jr. (*left*) also worked together in the 2020 movie *Dolittle*. Holland brought his dog, Tessa, to a showing of the movie in London.

TIMELINE

Thomas Stanley Holland was born on June 1 near London, England.

1996

Tom filmed the movie *The Impossible*.

2010

2008

Tom earned the starring role in *Billy Elliot: The Musical*.

Tom played a sailor in the movie In the Heart of the Sea.

2013

2014

Holland went to carpentry school.

Holland first appeared as Spider-Man in Captain America: Civil War.

2016

2017

Spider-Man: Homecoming was released.

Spider-Man: Far from Home was released.

2019

2020

Holland worked with Robert Downey Jr. in Dolittle.

29

GLOSSARY

audition (aw-DIH-shuhn)—a trial performance showcasing personal talent as a musician, a singer, a dancer, or an actor. Also, to give such a performance.

comedian—a person who uses funny speech and actions to make people laugh.

confident—having faith in your own abilities.

gymnastics—a sport that involves jumps, flips, and other athletic movements and exercises.

hip-hop—a form of popular music that features rhyme, spoken words, and electronic sounds. It is similar to rap music.

photographer (foh-TAH-gra-fur)—a person who takes pictures with a camera.

role—a part an actor plays.

script—the written text of a play, movie, or TV show.

tsunami (soo-NAH-mee)—a group of powerful ocean waves that can destroy large areas of land.

ONLINE RESOURCES

To learn more about Tom Holland, please visit **abdobooklinks.com** or scan this QR code. These links are routinely monitored and updated to provide the most current information available.

INDEX

Academy Awards, 26
Avengers: Endgame, 24, 26
Avengers: Infinity War, 24

Billy Elliot: The Musical, 8, 9, 10, 11, 28
birth, 6, 28

Captain America: Civil War, 20, 29
carpentry school, 14, 15, 16, 29
Chaos Walking, 25
childhood, 6, 8, 10, 11, 12, 13

dance, 6, 8, 10, 18
Dolittle, 27, 29
Downey, Robert, Jr., 16, 17, 27, 29

England, 4, 6, 9, 27, 28
Evans, Chris, 16

family, 6, 7

Hemsworth, Chris, 13
Howard, Ron, 13

Impossible, The, 12, 28
In the Heart of the Sea, 12, 13, 29

Maguire, Tobey, 21
Marvel Comics, 14
Marvel Studios, 18

New York City, 22

Ridley, Daisy, 25

Spider-Man (character), 4, 14, 16, 18, 19, 20, 21, 22, 24, 29
Spider-Man: Far from Home, 24, 29
Spider-Man: Homecoming, 22, 23, 29
superheroes, 4, 14, 16, 17, 18, 19, 20, 21, 22, 24, 29

theater, 8, 9, 10, 11, 12

Victoria Palace Theatre, 9

Wales, 15
Walker, Benjamin, 13
Watts, Jon, 23